MEDITATION - The Healing Response To TRAUMA

Kenneth S. Crowley

CONTENT

CHAPTER 1

Trauma Defined

Trauma is the reaction to a very upsetting or unsettling occurrence that overwhelms an individual's capacity to cope, generates feelings of helplessness, and limits their sense of self and their ability to feel a complete spectrum of emotions and experiences.

It does not discriminate and it is prevalent across the planet.

A World Mental Health study done by the World Health Organization indicated that at least a third of the more than 125,000 persons examined in 26 different nations had experienced trauma.

That figure grew to 70% when the sample was confined to persons having core illnesses as described by the DSM-IV (the categorization contained in the Diagnostic and Statistical Manual of Mental Disorders, 4th Edition) (the classification found in the Diagnostic and Statistical Manual of Mental Disorders, 4th Edition).

But those statistics are only for incidents that have been recorded; the true number is probably much, much greater.

While there are no objective criteria to identify whether events may create post-trauma symptoms, conditions often entail a loss of control, betrayal, misuse of power, helplessness, suffering, disorientation, and/or loss.

The incident need not reach the level of war, natural catastrophe, or personal attack to affect a person deeply and change their experiences.

Traumatic experiences that generate post-trauma symptoms differ pretty considerably from person to person.

Indeed, it is quite subjective and it is vital to keep in mind that it is characterized more by its reaction than its cause.

Common Responses And Symptoms Of Trauma

Response to a traumatic incident varies widely across persons, however, there are certain fundamental, typical signs.

Emotional indications include:

- Sadness
- Anger
- Denial
- Fear
- Shame

These may lead to:

- nightmares
- insomnia
- trouble with relationships
- emotional outbursts

Common physical symptoms:

- nausea
- dizziness
- changed sleep patterns
- changes in appetite
- headaches
- gastrointestinal troubles

Psychological problems may include:

- PTSD
- depression
- anxicty
- dissociative disorders
- drug abuse difficulties

Acute Stress Disorder Vs. Post-Traumatic Stress Disorder

Not every wounded individual gets post-traumatic stress disorder (PTSD).

Some individuals get some symptoms like those indicated above, but they disappear within a few weeks.
This is termed acute stress disorder (ASD).

When the symptoms endure longer than a month and substantially damage the individual's capacity to operate, the person may be suffering from PTSD.

Some persons with PTSD don't display symptoms for months.

What is PSTD

PTSD is a mental health problem that arises following exposure to a stressful experience.

The traumatic incident may be experienced f irst
hand, seen, or happen to someone close to y ou.

Some instances of catastrophic experiences are:

1. Serious accidents.
2. Military battle.
3. Natural calamities.
4. Personal attacks.
5. Abuse.

Not everyone who encounters a traumatic in cident will acquire PTSD, and a range of circ umstances may impact whether someone de velops it.

For example, women are more likely to expe rience PTSD than males.
Overall, 3.5% of U.S. adults suffer from PTSD.
However, this incidence is greater among mi litary veterans and individuals whose vocati

ons enhance the risk of exposure to traumati c events, such as firemen, emergency medic al workers, and police.

Symptoms

After a traumatic experience, a variety of sy mptoms must appear for the individual to fu lfill the criteria for a diagnosis of PTSD:

Intrusion symptoms.
At least 1 incursion symptom must be prese nt.

- Recurrent, involuntary, and unpleasan t recollections of the incident
- Frequent disturbing nightmares conce rning the incident
- Reactions, such as flashbacks, when o ne feels or behaves like the incident is occurring again
- Intense or long-lasting psychological a nguish after being exposed to items th at remind them of what transpired

- Physical responses to memories of the incident, such as a beating heart

Avoidance symptoms.
At least 1 avoidance symptom must be prese nt.

- Avoiding memories, thoughts, or emot ions relating to the event
- Avoiding reminders, such as people, pl aces, activities, talks, things, or circum stances that generate memories, thoug hts, or emotions associated with the ev ent

Cognitions and mood symptoms.
At least 2 negative changes in cognition and mood must be evident.

- lack of capacity to remember essential portions of the trauma
- Persistent and erroneous negative idea s about oneself, others, or the world
- Persistent, incorrect ideas about the ca use or repercussions of the occurrence , which generally causes a person to bl ame herself or others
- Consistently unpleasant emotional sta te
- Noticeably diminished interest or enga gement in activities
- Feelings of alienation from others
- Enduring inability to feel joyful emotio ns

<u>Arousal and reactivity symptoms</u>.

At least 2 observable modifications must be present.

- Irritability and rage

CHAPTER 2

Causes

PTSD is often induced by directly experiencing or witnessing a stressful incident. This may involve a single occurrence such as a catastrophic accident, attack, or abrupt death of a loved one. Repeated traumas throughout childhood might induce PTSD such as abuse or neglect. Combat scenarios like being tortured, held hostage, or imprisoned may also trigger PTSD. Less severe kinds of stress such as being divorced, being fired from a job, or failing in school don't generally trigger PTSD.

Diagnosis

A diagnosis of PTSD requires the patient to display particular sets of symptoms that continue for at least one month. These symptoms may be categorized into three broad types. The patient may reexperience the traumatic incident, which may take the form of flashbacks that occur while the patient is awake or nightmares while the patient is asleep. The patient may also suffer heightened physical or emotional responses to stimuli known as triggers.

The second group of symptoms for PTSD is avoidance behavior of objects that are associated with the traumatic experience. This also involves a lack of interest in connected activities or feelings of separation from other individuals. The third group of PTSD symptoms is an elevated degree of arousal, which includes sleeping trouble, issues with attention, impatience, and an amplified startle reaction.

Types

PTSD may be split into subtypes including acute, chronic, and delayed PTSD. The symptoms of acute PTSD endure between one to three months and substantially impede the patient's ability to operate. The diagnosis may be altered to chronic PTSD when the symptoms linger for more than three months.

Chronic PTSD is less likely to recover without therapy than acute PTSD, and these people should seek treatment quickly.

Delayed PTSD occurs when the symptoms reappear after being gone for at least several months. This recurrence commonly occurs on the anniversary of the incident that first triggered the PTSD or when the patient encounters a comparable occurrence.

Treatment

The therapies for PTSD may typically be separated between psychotherapy and medication. Some people react well to one therapy approach, while other individuals need both modalities. Psychotherapy is typically the best treatment for PTSD when the symptoms are moderate or when medication is prohibited, as is the case with pregnant or lactating women.

Some people may have a medical condition that limits the use of psychoactive medications used to treat PTSD. Medication is more likely to be the recommended therapy for PTSD when the symptoms are severe or chronic. Patients who have additional mental issues may also benefit from medication, particularly when psychotherapy has been unsuccessful by itself.

Psychotherapy

The most effective kinds of treatment for PTSD are anxiety control, cognitive therapy, and exposure therapy. Anxiety management provides patients with strategies that will help them deal with the symptoms of PTSD. These include relaxation training, breathing retraining, positive thinking, assertiveness training, and mind-stopping.

Cognitive therapy entails modifying the patient's erroneous ideas that interfere with psychological functioning and generate emotional problems. Exposure treatment requires the patient to address particular triggers that create the symptoms of PTSD. This might involve psychological exposure in the form of memories or physical exposure to genuine experiences. Play therapy may also be beneficial therapy for children with PTSD, in which youngsters play out their anxiety with enjoyable activities.

Medication

Selective serotonin reuptake inhibitors are the primary antidepressants for the medical treatment of PTSD. SSRIs now accessible in the United States include Zoloft, Paxil,

Prozac, Luvox, and Celexa. Other antidepressants that may be used when SSRIs are unsuccessful include Effexor. The next alternative of medicine for treating PTSD is the older tricyclic antidepressants such as Elavil, however, they have greater negative effects than the newer treatments.

A psychiatrist may also prescribe mood stabilizers such as Depakote if the patient displays a limited response to antidepressants. Mood stabilizers are most typically used to treat PTSD when the patient's major symptoms include strong anger or irritability. Patients are also likely to need mood stabilizers if they have bipolar disorder.

Antianxiety drugs such as benzodiazepines may be used to treat PTSD when anxiety is its most dominating symptom. The basic options are Valium, Xanax, Klonopin, and Ativan. Benzodiazepines should be used on a short-term basis owing to the likelihood of a reliance forming.

Family Support

Family members may be a vital component of a patient's rehabilitation from PTSD if they are excellent listeners and give emotional support. They must resist the temptation to just urge them to go on with their lives. Patients typically have the greatest chance of healing from PTSD when they get support from family members to discuss their recollections of the traumatic incident.

The family members of a PTSD patient may also assist the patient get rid of the guilt they frequently experience by reminding them they are not to blame and are not alone. Family members must also have reasonable expectations regarding a patient's recovery from PTSD while encouraging patients to seek exposure to triggers. Support groups are also a typical approach to helping patients and family members manage PTSD. These support groups are provided via several organizations.

Post-traumatic stress disorder (PTSD) is brought on by seeing a horrific, typically life-threatening, experience. Severe anxiety, flashbacks, uncontrolled thoughts, and nightmares are frequent signs of the condition. These symptoms may intensify and linger for years, therefore it is recommended to get treatment for PTSD as soon as possible.

Are There Different Types of PTSD?

Three main forms of post-traumatic stress disorder exist. If symptoms persist for fewer than three months, the disease is labeled acute PTSD. If symptoms linger for at least three months, the disease is referred to as chronic PTSD. If symptoms manifest at least six months following a traumatic event, the disorder is classified as delayed-onset PTSD, according to the National Institute of Health (NIH) (NIH).

What Causes PTSD?

Post-traumatic stress disorder is a mental health condition that is triggered when a person witnesses a psychologically traumatic event, such as war, a natural disaster, or any situation that invokes feelings of helplessness or intense fear. While most people eventually adjust to the aftereffects of such events, some people find their symptoms getting worse with time. These worsening symptoms are the product of PTSD.

As is usually the case with mental health issues, doctors cannot pinpoint why some people develop PTSD. According to the Mayo Clinic, probable causes of PTSD include inherited mental and personality traits, a culmination of life experiences, and the way hormones and chemicals are regulated by the brain when responding to stress.

What Are the Signs of PTSD?

The Mayo Clinic mentions several reoccurring symptoms, including fearful thoughts, flashbacks, and bad dreams. These symptoms can become problematic in a person's life. Some of the avoidance symptoms include difficulty remembering the traumatic event and avoiding reminders of the experience, such as places, people, and objects.

Hyperarousal symptoms may also arise, such as feeling tense, being startled easily, and having trouble sleeping. While it is normal to experience some of these symptoms after a terrible event, symptoms lasting more than a few weeks may be signs of PTSD.

Emotional Symptoms of PTSD

The emotional symptoms of PTSD are depression, worry, intense guilt, and feeling emotionally numb. Another symptom is anhedonia, which is characterized by a loss of interest in formerly enjoyable activities. The National Center for Biotechnology Information (NCBI) states that anhedonia plays a part in predicting psychiatric comorbidity, or the presence of more than one psychiatric disorder.

Physical Symptoms of PTSD

The NCBI has documented many physical complaints among PTSD sufferers. The physical problems reported included higher rates of neurological, respiratory, musculoskeletal, and cardiovascular symptoms. Feelings of depression, guilt, tension, worry, and difficulty sleeping may contribute to physical ailments.

Short-Term and Long-Term Effects of PTSD

Post-traumatic stress disorder causes short-term memory loss and can have long-term chronic psychological repercussions, according to the American Psychological Association (APA) and the NCBI. Fortunately, psychotherapeutic intervention and treatment can alleviate and often eliminate short-term and long-term effects of PTSD.

Is There a Test or Self-Assessment I Can Do?

There are free, anonymous self-assessments accessible online, such as this exam sponsored by the Anxiety and Depression Association of America. You should discuss your findings with your doctor, or you may contact us for further information.

Post-Traumatic Stress Disorder Medication: PTSD Drug Options

Per the NIH, the United States Food and Drug Administration has authorized sertraline (Zoloft) and paroxetine (Paxil), both antidepressants, for use as post-traumatic stress disorder medicine. The adverse effects of these medications include:

Headache
Nausea
Sleeplessness or drowsiness
Agitation or a restless sensation
Problems having or enjoying sex\sMost of these symptoms tend to fade within a short amount of time.

PTSD Drugs: Possible Options
Doctors may give drugs other than Zoloft and Paxil, particularly if comorbid conditions occur. According to the NIH, benzodiazepines are used to help with relaxation and sleep. The negative effects include issues with memory and the danger of drug dependence. Antipsychotics may be prescribed. They are often administered to individuals with comorbid illnesses, such as schizophrenia. Some negative effects of antipsychotics include weight gain and an

increased risk of heart disease and diabetes. Additionally, various antidepressants may be utilized as PTSD medicines. Possible possibilities include fluoxetine (Prozac) and citalopram (Celexa) (Celexa).

Medication Side Effects

In addition to the negative effects previously stated, the following side effects may occur:

Dry mouth
Increased appetite
Blurred vision
Dizziness

Some antidepressants have a greater probability of causing weight gain than others. Nausea and headaches normally cease occurring after a few weeks of taking the drugs. For dry mouth, chew gum or suck on ice cubes. If you suffer from sleepiness, take your prescription before bedtime. Likewise, for insomnia, take your prescription in the morning. Drink a lot of water to prevent constipation, and stop the usage of cigarettes, alcohol, and caffeine to minimize dizziness. Talk to your doctor about how your medicine affects you. There may be solutions that are better suited if you find the side effects of a certain drug overpowering.

PTSD Drug Addiction, Dependence and Withdrawal

The Journal of the American Academy of Family Physicians cautions about the misuse danger of benzodiazepines. When used chronically, they may be addicting yet they are reasonably safe when taken in moderation. If you have a history of drug misuse, benzodiazepines should not be utilized. It is crucial that you not quit taking your medicine as this might create withdrawal effects and lead to a return of the symptoms of your condition. Instead, ask your doctor about weaning you off the medicine. Always inform your doctor about your drug concerns so you may arrange an alternate PTSD treatment program.

Medication Overdose

Overdosing should not be a worry if the medicine is used just as recommended. The National Safety Council suggests that you never take a larger daily dose than suggested by your doctor and that you not refill your prescriptions early. Avoid alcohol or sedatives while taking drugs, and inform your doctor about any additional medications you are taking. Always store drugs in their original packaging.

Read the pamphlets that come with your drugs to acquaint yourself with side effects, indicators of toxicity, what to do if you miss a dose and what to do in the event of medication overdose. If you have any questions, consult your doctor or pharmacist. If you fear you may have overdosed, go to the emergency hospital immediately.

CHAPTER 3

Depression and PTSD

Depression is defined by feelings of melancholy or poor mood lasting longer than a few days. Depression and PTSD frequently occur concurrently. Almost one in 10 American people suffer from depression in a given year, according to the United States Department of Veterans Affairs. Depression may damage your capacity to conduct everyday duties and can reduce your quality of life. It also has harmful impacts on eating and sleeping patterns.

Depression is three to five times more likely to be diagnosed in those who are living with

PTSD. If you no longer care about things you formerly loved or are experiencing thoughts of suicide or injuring yourself, get treatment immediately. We are available any time and can be reached at.

Dual Diagnosis: Addiction and PTSD

Studies done by the National Center for Post-Traumatic Stress Disorder indicated a substantial association between drug use problems and PTSD. For patients suffering from these co-occurring disorders, studies suggest keeping detailed journals of your feelings, thoughts, and behaviors and then talking to your doctor about them. Be sure to discuss issues you may be having with substance abuse and PTSD, as a big deterrent in the efficacy of treatment is the tendency to focus only on the condition that seems to be bothering the patient most. Communicating with your doctor is of the utmost importance in treating any disorder.

Post-traumatic stress disorder is a condition that affects millions of Americans every year. Government statistics indicate that 3.5 percent of the general population suffers from PTSD. The disorder is strongly associated with soldiers due to the many instances of traumatic events they endure while at war, but the label can be applied to anyone who experiences the effects of trauma. The individual may have experienced the trauma personally or may have the condition as a result of a traumatic event that happened to a loved one. It is not uncommon for people to develop PTSD after the death of a family member.

What Causes PTSD?

Post-traumatic stress disorder is caused by significant trauma in a person's life that is left unresolved. While PTSD is often linked with veterans of the military, anybody who has suffered stress in life might get PTSD at any age. PTSD is described as an anxiety condition in which a person's natural reaction to a threat becomes perverted. After going through a traumatic experience, the affected person may be activated and have a fight-or-flight reaction long after the event has gone.

Fight-or-flight responses are natural, but when they are triggered by daily events, the results can be debilitating and even dangerous. It is crucial to get help for PTSD symptoms that last longer than six to eight weeks. After eight weeks, the symptoms are likely permanent and will only worsen with time if they are allowed to continue without medical intervention. Like other mental disorders, PTSD responds well to treatment, and affected individuals can look forward to positive results once treatment begins.

Is There a Cure for PTSD?

As with most mental illnesses, no cure exists for PTSD, but the symptoms can be effectively managed to restore the affected individual to normal functioning. The best hope for treating PTSD is a combination of medication and therapy. By engaging with a healthcare expert, persons with PTSD may address their triggering circumstances and learn new and effective methods of living with the stress of the prior trauma.

Don't Face This Alone. Private, Professional Online Therapy Can Help You.
Find The Right Therapist For You Today

Therapies for PTSD

Numerous treatments are available for the treatment of post-traumatic stress disorder. Some of the most frequent techniques used to treat PTSD include group therapy, psychotherapy, cognitive behavioral therapy, and hypnosis. In certain circumstances, physicians may propose a mix of one or more therapy modalities to fulfill the requirements of the specific patient.

In general, no right or wrong strategy exists when it comes to the treatment of PTSD. Some people react better to specific therapies than others. The efficiency of a certain therapy relies on various aspects, including the individual's personality, the type of trauma, the intensity of the symptoms, and the availability of a support network. While numerous kinds of successful therapy exist for PTSD, certain therapies have been demonstrated to be more beneficial for the whole population than others.

PTSD therapy is focused on treating the symptoms of the disease and assisting the afflicted person to better comprehend the reasons. Some frequent symptoms that influence the lives of persons living with PTSD include:

- Night terrors
- Flashbacks
- Avoidance
- Emotional numbness
- Indifference

These symptoms may create tremendous disruption in an individual's life, but the government believes that a huge 50 percent of persons who have PTSD do not seek treatment. Individuals with PTSD do not seek therapy for numerous reasons, ranging from fear of judgment to an inability to bear the fees.

If you or a loved one is suffering from the symptoms of PTSD, do not wait any longer; our hotline is open 24/7, and we can chat with you about all the various choices you may pick when it comes to seeking assistance for your PTSD. Call us any time for further information or just to chat with someone who knows what you are going through.

Cognitive Behavioral Therapy Treatments

Cognitive behavioral therapy is an increasingly common style of treatment that originally became widely recognized in the 1980s. It mixes the ideas of cognitive psychology and behavioral therapy to produce a holistic therapeutic method. The cognitive part focuses on the ways the human capacity to problem-solve and think logically might promote healing. The behavioral part focuses on how the health of the mind appears via human behavior.

Most cognitive behavioral therapists will concentrate on helping the PTSD patient come to terms with the traumatic incident and then identify methods to adjust behavior to deal more effectively.

Other Therapeutic Methods

Group therapy is another prominent therapeutic approach for persons with PTSD. The fundamental advantage of group therapy is it helps victims of trauma to connect with people who understand what they have gone through. That understanding is especially crucial for victims of violent crimes who may feel alienated from their peers owing to the rare nature of their experiences. Group therapy gives a secure space to address the traumatic experiences as well as any associated thoughts and behaviors without fear of judgment from people who have not gone through a similar experience.

Another prominent therapeutic strategy is hypnotherapy, but this kind of treatment is often used in combination with established treatments. Hypnosis is frequently used to assist the patient cope with the trauma by regressing to a condition before its occurrence and to utilize the power of the mind to overcome any resultant behavioral difficulties.

Residential Inpatient PTSD Treatment Centers

If you or a loved one is suffering from a post-traumatic stress disorder and wishes to seek therapy, residential or inpatient PTSD treatment clinics are a viable alternative. These institutions are staffed by skilled professionals who can analyze your illness and design the best treatment plan for you in a setting that is as stress-free as possible.

The Benefits of Residential PTSD Treatment

One of the most challenging parts of living with PTSD is the fact that the person might easily be triggered by regular situations. Gunfire, fireworks, bright lights, and other typical events that are upsetting to the senses might transfer someone with PTSD back to the condition they were in when the incident happened. These flashbacks generally occur at night when the individual is sleeping, but they may occur at any moment, drastically disturbing the flow of regular life.

A residential treatment facility provides patients the chance to recuperate in an atmosphere that is free from the rigors of regular life and surrounded by specialists who understand the nature of what they are going through. If you would like more information about PTSD rehabilitation clinics, contact our toll-free helpline for more information now.

Luxury PTSD Facilities

When most people visualize a PTSD treatment center, they don't expect a nice and calm place. Many premium PTSD clinics provide this kind of ambiance, where patients may rest in surroundings that match those of the top luxury resorts.

Executive PTSD Programs

Like luxury PTSD facilities, executive PTSD programs offer a high-class treatment experience. For the busy executive who wants to put the effort into recovery but just doesn't have the time to be completely disconnected from the office, luxury treatment centers offer a great compromise. You can receive treatment in a luxurious facility while having access to the technology you need to stay connected to your work.

Outpatient PTSD Rehab and Treatment Programs

For those whose schedules will not allow for an inpatient treatment program, outpatient PTSD rehab and treatment programs are a great option. These facilities are staffed by knowledgeable healthcare professionals who can help you take the lessons you learn in treatment and transfer them to life at home and work.

<u>Prescription and Over-the-Counter Medications</u>

Prescription medications are commonly prescribed to treat the symptoms of post-traumatic stress disorder and make living with the disorder more manageable.

Self-medication with over-the-counter medication can be dangerous, and you should consult your doctor before taking any medication for the treatment of your PTSD symptoms. Over-the-counter medication may be readily available, but taking the wrong medication at the wrong dosage can make your PTSD symptoms worse, and the practice is also dangerous.

PTSD and drug misuse regrettably have a high likelihood of comorbidity. The Department of Veterans Affairs states that 20 percent of persons who suffer from PTSD also suffer from a drug misuse issue. Many victims of trauma resort to drugs or alcohol to deal with the symptoms of PTSD and to escape the perceived stigma of seeking therapy. Substance misuse may appear to be a way out in the beginning, but the incorrect use of drugs and alcohol to treat PTSD may only hide the symptoms for a brief period. To achieve meaningful healing, it is vital to get professional therapy from a competent mental health practitioner. Attempts at self-medication with either prescription drugs or over-the-counter medications will only lead to more problems and deeper depression.

Treatment centers are prepared to deal with patients who suffer from PTSD and substance abuse. They employ some treatment methods such as cognitive behavioral therapies, cognitive processing therapy and prescription drugs to assist cope with PTSD or substance misuse symptoms.

How to Find the Best PTSD Treatment Facility

When it comes to locating a PTSD treatment center for yourself or a loved one, you want the best. Many fantastic treatment facilities are staffed with skilled mental health specialists who are eager to assist you to accomplish your treatment objectives. It is possible to live a normal life with PTSD by controlling the symptoms and having a strong network of support. Some tools are better than others, however, and the sheer diversity of information on the Internet may be daunting at times.

Post-traumatic stress disorder is a hard illness, and healing is a long-term objective rather than something that can be reached instantly. Fortunately, support is one of the most powerful strategies available when it comes to addressing the causes and symptoms of PTSD. A solid network of family and friends is vital to the rehabilitation process, but it is also necessary to engage closely with a mental health expert who can monitor your progress and well-being.

It's crucial to obtain aid in treating Post-traumatic stress disorder for you or your loved one. Call us now for more details.

Estimates show that up to 70 percent of American adults have encountered at least one serious trauma over their careers. Many of those persons may afterward have suffered from an emotional response known as posttraumatic stress disorder or PTSD. Further estimates show that 5 percent of the population today lives with PTSD.

What Is PTSD?

Posttraumatic stress disorder happens in certain circumstances when individuals are subjected to a particularly stressful incident, which is known as an excessive stress trigger. To be diagnosed with PTSD, people must continue to have symptoms of PTSD for at least one month following exposure to this trigger.

Who Experiences PTSD?

Although women are twice as likely as males to acquire PTSD, anybody who endures an extraordinarily stressful incident may develop posttraumatic stress disorder. Examples of high-stress triggers include:

- Criminal assault or rape
- Natural catastrophes
- Serious accidents
- Combat exposure
- Child physical or sexual abuse or severe neglect
- Witnessing horrific occurrences
- Imprisonment/hostage/displacement as refugees
- Torture
- The abrupt unexpected death of loved ones

Although other forms of stress may be intense and might be highly unpleasant, they normally do not result in PTSD. Such circumstances could include the death of an aging parent, divorce, or job loss.

What Are the Symptoms of PTSD?

People living with PTSD typically experience three main types of symptoms. First, individuals may reexperience the terrible incident that contributed to developing PTSD. This might include:

Flashbacks in which they feel that the triggering event is recurring even while they are awake
Distressing memories of the horrific incident
Nightmares of the event
Exaggerated physical and emotional responses to cues that remind them of the incident
The second sort of symptom includes emotional numbness or even avoidance. It may involve the following symptoms or behaviors:

Avoidance of locations, ideas, activities, conversations, and sensations associated with the incident or trauma
Feelings of separation
Loss of interest
Restricted emotions

The third symptom type refers to heightened arousal associated with the incident and may be characterized by:

- Outbursts of fury
- Irritability
- Difficulty sleeping
- Hypervigilance
- Difficulty concentrating
- Exaggerated startle responses

Related Conditions and Problems

In addition to the symptoms described above, patients with PTSD may suffer an array of additional symptoms. With appropriate therapy, many of these symptoms will improve. The individual with PTSD may need further therapy to address the entire array of symptoms associated with PTSD.

Panic Attacks

People who have endured substantial trauma may develop panic attacks when they are exposed to a trigger that reminds them of the instigating event. For instance, someone who gets PTSD as a consequence of military exposure may experience a panic episode upon hearing a loud noise that reminds them of an explosion. During a panic attack, the sufferer will usually feel acute discomfort or terror. This may be accompanied by psychological or physical symptoms, which could include:

- Sweating
- Racing or thumping heart
- Soreness of breath
- Shaking or trembling
- Dizziness
- Nausea
- Chest pain
- Numbness
- Hot flushes
- Tingling

People may have a sensation of separation or may even feel as if they are dying, going insane, or experiencing heart attacks.

Severe Avoidance Behavior

One of the most typical symptoms of PTSD is avoidance of anything that reminds the individual of the initial incident. Avoidance may occasionally extend to regular circumstances. In certain circumstances, this sort of avoidance becomes so extreme that the person is unable to leave his or her house.

Depression

Many persons suffering from PTSD also feel depressed. They may be unable to take pleasure or interest in activities they formerly liked. Unjustified sentiments of self-blame or guilt are widespread.

Suicidal Thoughts

In some situations, depression may become so severe that the person with PTSD develops thoughts of suicide because of beliefs that life is just not worth continuing.

Substance Abuse

People with PTSD may also use drugs or alcohol in an attempt to dull the agony they are feeling. They may abuse over-the-counter medicines or prescription drugs. This substance abuse can magnify the symptoms of PTSD.

Treatments for PTSD

There are two basic forms of treatment available for PTSD: psychotherapy and medication. Some individuals can completely recover from posttraumatic stress disorder utilizing psychotherapy alone, whereas others require a mix of both therapies to achieve full recovery.

Psychotherapy alone is generally helpful for those who suffer minor symptoms, those who should not take medication due to pregnancy or because they are nursing, and persons who choose not to use medication.

Medication may be a useful choice for persons with severe symptoms or those who have lived with their symptoms for a long period. People who have other psychological disorders such as anxiety or depression may also need medication.

Psychotherapy

Professionals may employ three forms of psychotherapy while treating PTSD: cognitive therapy, anxiety management, and exposure treatment. If they are treating youngsters with PTSD, they may also employ play therapy. During anxiety treatment, patients learn how to better deal with their symptoms via relaxation training, breathing retraining, and positive thinking and self-talk. Therapists may educate patients on how to regulate their anxiety and terror by relaxing the primary muscle groups in their body, one at a time. To cope with hyperventilation, therapists educate patients on how to employ slow breathing strategies to battle tingling, dizziness, and palpitations. During positive thinking and self-talk, therapists encourage clients to replace negative ideas with good ones when they are presented with memories of the initial trauma. Therapists may also utilize assertiveness training to educate patients on how to express their feelings without driving others away.

Medication

Several forms of drugs are available to assist treat someone with posttraumatic stress disorder. These include antidepressants, mood stabilizers, and antianxiety medicines.

People with acute PTSD who have had symptoms for fewer than three months may require medication for between six and 12 months. Individuals with chronic PTSD who have had symptoms for longer than three months may need medication for a minimum of one year. In some instances, people may relapse and begin to experience symptoms after they have ceased therapy and stopped taking medication. This can happen even years after the end of the treatment. If this happens, they may need to resume psychotherapy and medication.

www.ingramcontent.com/pod-product-compliance
Lightning Source LLC
LaVergne TN
LVHW052104160826
845678LV00015B/3355

* 9 7 9 8 3 6 5 4 8 2 9 2 0 *